Short and Tall

by Rod Theodorou and Carole Telford

Contents

Heinemann

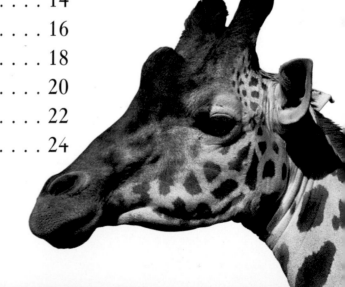

First published in Great Britain by Heinemann Library
an imprint of Heinemann Publishers (Oxford) Ltd
Halley Court, Jordan Hill, Oxford OX2 8EJ

MADRID ATHENS PARIS FLORENCE PRAGUE WARSAW
PORTSMOUTH NH CHICAGO SAO PAULO SINGAPORE TOKYO
MELBOURNE AUCKLAND IBADAN GABORONE JOHANNESBURG

Illustrations by Sheila Townsend and Trevor Dunton
Colour reproduction by Track QSP
Printed in China

99 98 97 96
10 9 8 7 6 5 4 3 2 1

ISBN 0 431 06395 8

British Library Cataloguing in Publication Data
Telford, Carole
 Short and Tall. – (Animal Opposites Series)
 I. Title II. Theodorou, Rod III. Series
 591

Photographic acknowledgements
Attilio Calegari/OSF(Oxford Scientific Films) pp4, 6 *bottom left*; Johnny Johnson/Bruce Coleman Ltd p5;
Norbert Rosing/OSF p7; Presstige Pictures/OSF p6 *top*; Barrie Watts/OSF pp6 *bottom right*, 10;
Philip Sharpe/OSF pp8, 13; Mark Deeble and Victoria Stone/OSF p9; M. Wendler Okapia/OSF p11;
Jim Hallet/OSF p12; Mark Hamblin/OSF p14; Rafi Ben-Shahar/OSF pp15, 19, 21; Tim Shepherd/OSF p20;
Terry Button/OSF p16;
Richard Packwood/OSF p17; Stouffer Enterprises Inc. Animals Animals/OSF p18
Front cover: Attilio Calegari/OSF; Eckart Pott/Bruce Coleman Ltd; Trevor Clifford

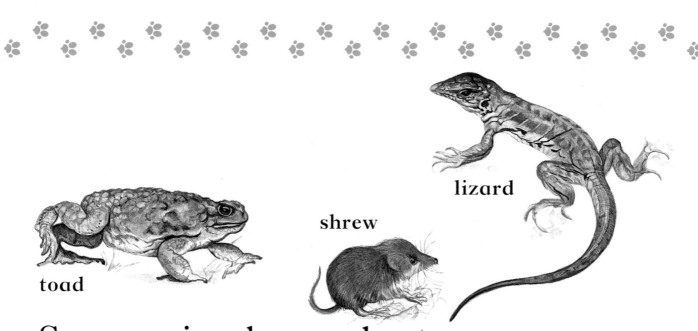

toad

shrew

lizard

Some animals are short.
Some animals are tall.

ostrich

camel

giraffe

This animal is a shrew.
A shrew is so tiny and short, it could sit in the palm of your hand.

This animal is
a giraffe.
A giraffe is large
and tall.
It can grow as
high as a
double-decker
bus.

5

There are shrews all over
the world.
Some live in warm countries.
Some live in cold countries.

water shrew

common shrew

6

pygmy shrew

Giraffes live in Africa.
They live in groups called herds.

Shrews live among leaves and grass.
They can wriggle through
small spaces.

Giraffes
live out in
the open.
Their spots
can help them
stay hidden
from their
enemies.

Shrews can see and smell very well.
They can watch out for their enemies.

Giraffes are so
tall they can see
a long way.
Giraffes watch
out for lions.

11

Shrews can hide from their
enemies in small holes.

Giraffes can run fast and
kick their enemies.

Many bigger animals hunt shrews.
This owl has killed a shrew.

Only big, fierce animals like
lions can kill a giraffe.

Shrews eat insects and other
small animals.
This shrew is eating a worm.

Giraffes
eat leaves.
They can
eat leaves
other animals
cannot reach.

A shrew has lots of babies.
They need to grow fur to keep warm.

A giraffe
has one
baby a year.
When it is
born it has
a long way
to drop.

Baby shrews are safe in their nest.
When they grow bigger, they have
to leave the nest.

A baby giraffe has nowhere
safe to hide.
It must quickly learn to run.

AMAZING FACTS!

When a mother shrew leaves
the nest for food, her babies
follow her.
They hold onto each other's tails!

A baby giraffe can run with its mother only 10 hours after it is born!

A giraffe has to spread its legs to drink water.

Index